SOCCER STARS

COLORING BOOK

XBTO

2023 2024

SPORTZ ART CREATIONS

2

Thank you for buying the book! As gratitude for your support, I have a gift for you: a printable book with 25 images of player poses to design their kits.

I hope you enjoy it!

4

SECTION I

APPLYING THE COLORS OF EACH TEAM'S JERSEYS

INDEX

LEO MESSI

CRISTIANO RONALDO

11

JUDE BELLINGHAM

15

GABRIEL JESUS

17

CHRISTOPHER NKUNKU

19

DARWIN NUNEZ

21

VIRGIL VAN DIJK

23

ERLING HAALAND

25

MARCUS RASHFORD

27

HARRY KANE

29

JOSHUA KIMMICH

31

MANUEL NEUER

33

MARCO REUS

35

DONNARUMMA

37

LAUTARO MARTINEZ

VLAHOVIC

43

RAFAEL LEAO

45

DYBALA

47

SECTION II

CREATE YOUR OWN CUSTOMIZED JERSEY DESIGNS FOR EACH TEAM

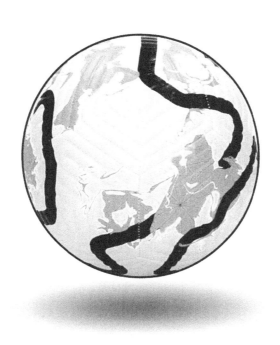

LEO MESSI

51

CRISTIANO RONALDO

53

LEWANDOWSKI

55

JUDE BELLINGHAM

GABRIEL JESUS

59

CHRISTOPHER NKUNKU

61

DARWIN NUNEZ

63

VIRGIL VAN DIJK

65

ERLING HAALAND

MARCUS RASHFORD

69

HARRY KANE

71

JOSHUA KIMMICH

73

MANUEL NEUER

75

MARCO REUS

77

DONNARUMMA

KYLIAN MBAPPE

81

LAUTARO MARTINEZ

VLAHOVIC

85

RAFAEL LEAO

DYBALA

89

I hope you've enjoyed the book. If you liked it, please consider leaving a positive review on Amazon and your feedback so that we can continue to improve.

We greatly appreciate your comments and will be happy to implement your recommendations.

sportzartcreations@gmail.com

Made in the USA
Las Vegas, NV
21 November 2024

12277272R00052